OXFORD
First Book
of
Art

Gillian Wolfe

OXFORD
UNIVERSITY PRESS

OXFORD
UNIVERSITY PRESS

198 Madison Avenue, New York, NY 10016

Oxford New York

Athens Auckland Bangkok Bogotá Buenos Aires Calcutta
Cape Town Chennai Dar es Salaam Delhi Florence Hong Kong Istanbul
Karachi Kuala Lumpur Madrid Melbourne Mexico City Mumbai
Nairobi Paris São Paulo Singapore Taipei Tokyo Toronto Warsaw

with associated companies in Berlin Ibadan

Oxford is a registered trade mark of Oxford University Press

Library of Congress Cataloguing-in-Publication data available

ISBN: 0-19-521556-7 (hardcover); 0-19-514577-1 (paperback)

3 5 7 9 10 8 6 4 2

Designed by White Design

Reclining Figure,
1951, *by Henry
Moore*

Contents

How to use this book

In this book there are paintings, drawings, weavings and sculptures.

Some of them were made a long time ago,

and some were made quite recently.

They come from all around the world,

and were made by artists of all kinds. But when these artists were children they drew and made imaginative art – just like you!

The pictures in the book are grouped together under headings, so that you can see how different artists have made pictures about a particular topic.

You can find out about each picture by reading the description next to it.

Mother and Child

The Naughty Boy, *by Hubert von Herkomer*

A pretty country cottage, overgrown with roses and creepers, is the background for a family scene. An **angry** mother lifts up her *naughty* boy, and her head is turned away as she furiously tells someone behind her what he has done. The little boy looks uncomfortable as he is held roughly under the arms. Neither of them looks happy.

The infant Jesus is **frightened** by a fluttering bird, which young St John holds out to him. He turns to his mother Mary for comfort. The scene is carved out of a stone called marble, but the artist did not finish it. Can you see where Michelangelo's chisel cut the stone *roughly* at the outer edges? He then used a smaller chisel to chip *d e l i c a t e l y* at the figures.

Madonna and Child, *by Michelangelo Buonarroti*

This artist loved to paint mothers with their children. She captured their most **tender** moments together. Bath-time is ordinary and everyday, yet here we feel that we are allowed to *p e e p* in on an especially private moment. Mother and child gaze downwards, absorbed in the washing of small feet.

Before there were bathrooms and running water from taps, people used to pour water from a large jug into a wide china bowl to wash. Here the jug and the bowl are on the floor, so that the child can dip her toes in the water.

Look closer

- Can you see a shadowy person in the doorway of the cottage in *The Naughty Boy*?
- When you look at *The Bath*, do you seem to be looking up at the two people or down at them?
- Can you find three different patterns in *The Bath* picture? Which part is not patterned?
- Which are the smoothest parts of the sculpture of the *Madonna and Child*?

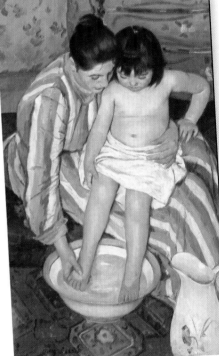

The Child's Bath, *by Mary Cassatt*

Activity

Make a splashy, watery painting of *you* being washed, showered or bathed. Show whether you enjoy it or not!

Under the "Look Closer" heading there are questions for you to answer. They will help you to become really involved in what's going on in the pictures.

Where you see this hand sign, you will find an art "Activity" to try on your own. Each one suggests ways in which you can use ideas in the artists' work in your own pictures.

At the end of the book there is a chance for you to be an art detective! You will find collections of details from many of the pictures. How sharp are your eyes? Can you find where the details come from?

Mother and Child

The Naughty Boy,
*by Hubert von
Herkomer*

A pretty country cottage, overgrown with roses and creepers, is the
background for a family scene. An ***angry*** mother lifts up her ***naughty***
boy, and her head is turned away as she furiously tells someone behind
her what he has done. The little boy looks uncomfortable as he is held
roughly under the arms. Neither of them looks happy.

The infant Jesus is ***frightened*** by a fluttering bird,
which young St John holds out to him. He turns to his
mother Mary for comfort. The scene is carved out of
a stone called marble, but the artist did not finish it.
Can you see where Michelangelo's chisel cut the
stone ***roughly*** at the outer edges? He then used a
smaller chisel to chip ***delicately*** at the figures.

Madonna and Child,
by Michelangelo Buonarroti

This artist loved to paint mothers with their children. She captured their most **tender** moments together. Bathtime is ordinary and everyday, yet here we feel that we are allowed to **peep** in on an especially private moment. Mother and child gaze downwards, absorbed in the washing of small feet.

Before there were bathrooms and running water from faucets, people used to pour water from a large jug into a wide china bowl to wash. Here the jug and the bowl are on the floor, so that the child can dip her toes in the water.

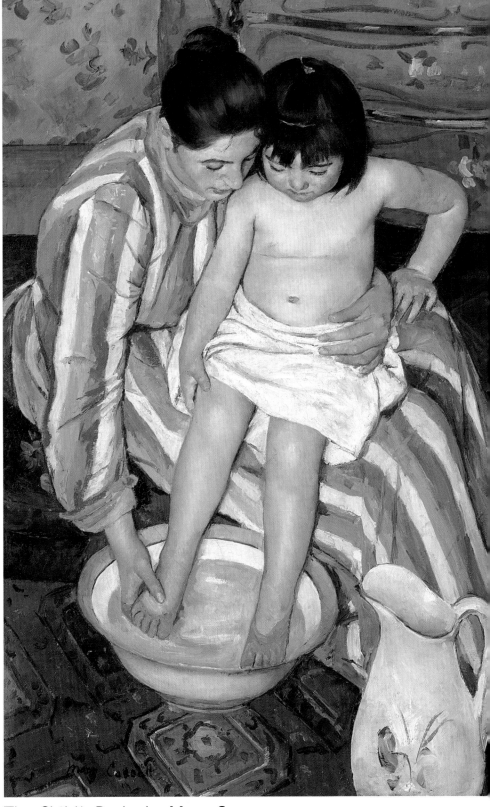

The Child's Bath, *by Mary Cassatt*

Look closer

- Can you see a shadowy person in the doorway of the cottage in *The Naughty Boy*?

- When you look at *The Child's Bath*, do you seem to be looking up at the two people or down at them?

- Can you find three different patterns in *The Child's Bath*? Which part is not patterned?

- Which are the smoothest parts of the sculpture of the *Madonna and Child*?

Activity

Make a splashy, watery painting of *you* being washed, showered, or bathed. Show whether you enjoy it or not!

Faces

Portrait of a Lady in Yellow,
by Alesso Baldovinetti

A side view of a head like this is called a **profile** portrait. This picture is very obviously of a real person. Her pale and delicate face has a crisp, clear outline. The artist has paid great attention to **detail**. See how each strand of hair stands out against the blue background, and how boldly the black leaf design shows up on her yellow-spotted sleeve.

Three-Faced Mask,
Ekoi people, Nigeria

Look closer

- Where else, in everyday things, can you see a head in profile?
- Can you find other carefully painted details in the profile portrait?
- How would you describe the different way that the two faces have been painted?
- Did you spot a sideways figure-eight shape in the picture by Klee?

This is an **all-around view** of a head. It has a face on three sides. It can look in all directions at once, to see, hear, and understand everything. Its three faces can also look into the past, the present, and the future.

Senecio, *by Paul Klee*

▲ This is a **front view** of a face. It is made up of lots of different shapes. Can you find circles, rectangles, squares, ovals, and a triangle? This is also a portrait of a real person, but the artist has not tried to make his face look **realistic**. The person was a performer, who wore a multicolored costume called a **harlequin**. See how the shapes in the face are like the shapes in the harlequin costume.

Activity

Draw a face using only circles or using only squares or rectangles, or using only triangles. Then make a face with a mixture of shapes, and color it in gorgeous colors.

11

Figures

Man Pointing,
*by Alberto
Giacometti*

⌕ Look closer

- Looking at all three pictures, which words would you use to describe which figure: slender, stiff, massive, rough-textured, weighty?
- The thin figure of the *Man Pointing* is made of a metal called bronze. Do you think it looks heavy?
- Why do you think the artist has not used many curves in the soldier painting?
- Can you find the figure of a queen in *Trooping the Colour*? How has the artist made her look different from all the other figures?

▶ This figure points with his right hand and seems to beckon with his left. When this artist modeled his figures he said that he looked for the "**bones under the skin**." This figure certainly looks thin and bony, like a stick man. His body is much longer than it would be in real life. This makes it look very *fragile*, as if it could break easily.

▶ The artist who made this drawing of a woman is famous for his sculptures. You can see how even in this sketch, he is thinking of the figure as if it were a sculpture. Look at the way his pen strokes make her seem **solid**, rounded, and as **HEAVY** as stone.

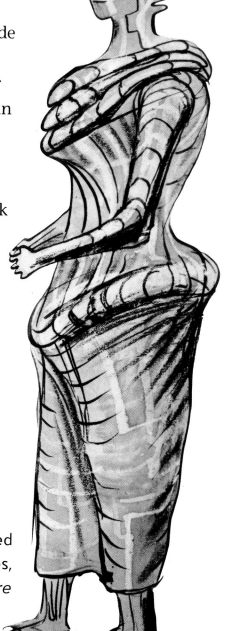

Detail from Draped Standing Figures,
by Henry Moore

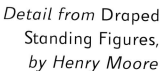

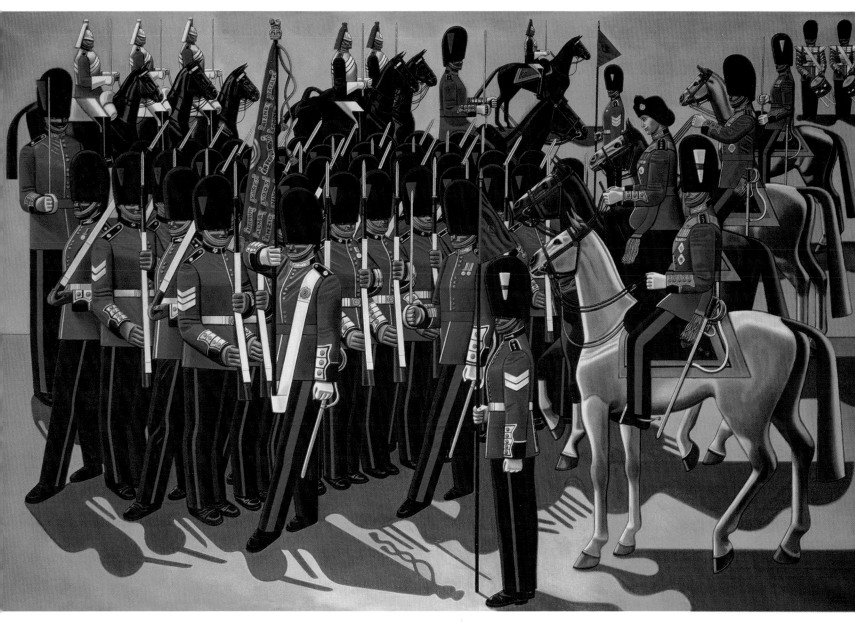

Trooping the Colour, *by William Roberts*

▲ Every year in London, soldiers carrying regimental flags (called "colors") march to celebrate the queen's birthday. Here the queen inspects the troops who have gathered in her honor. All the figures are *stiff* and *straight*. Guns, swords, arms, legs, flagpoles, and even stripes on uniforms are all painted in *vertical* lines, to add to the strong and *upright* look of the scene.

Activity

Use modeling clay to make some HEAVY, **stone-like** sculptures of people. Then, as a contrast, use pipe cleaners to make some *thin, wiry* people.

▶ The men almost look as if they have been made by a machine, like toy soldiers.

Moving Figures

The Mud Bath, *by David Bomberg*

At first glance you might think that these shapes have *nothing* to do with people. Look carefully and you will see that these are shapes of people *jostling* each other as they gather around a steam bath. This artist enjoyed the excitement and power of machines, and here the movements of the figures almost suggest parts of a **throbbing** machine at work.

Look closer

- Can you find the shapes of people leaping and diving in *The Mud Bath*?
- Klee's figure does not look solid. How is the way he shows movement different from Bomberg's?
- The athlete is made of a hard shiny stone called marble. Can you imagine how difficult it was to carve this whole figure from one single block of stone?

Paul Klee drew this **dancing** figure with one continuous long line, one squiggle, two dots, and a dash! With your finger, follow the line all the way round and see how he did it. The picture is full of *energy* and *movement*.

Activity

Take a line for a walk! Practice making the shape of a person without ever taking your pencil off the paper. This is a very good way to capture quick movements.

Discus Thrower, *ancient Rome*

Tanzt Entsetzen, *by Paul Klee*

In ancient times Greek and Roman sculptors studied the way our muscles work, to make their figures look as lifelike as possible. It was a real challenge to show an athlete in this difficult pose. Look at how the shoulders and hips slope downwards, the legs point forwards, while the chest and head twist sideways, towards us. Yet the figure is perfectly *balanced*. *You* try to take up this tricky pose!

15

Working

The Builders, *by Fernand Léger*

◀ Look at the way the artist has used dots and stripes as a **pattern** in this picture.

Large hands and strong muscles enable these builders to lift a **massive** iron girder into place on this building site. Look through the **hard**, straight lines of ladders and iron bars to the contrasting **soft** clouds floating in a clear sunny sky. Leger always liked to use really **bright** colors in his pictures.

Activity

Make a pattern picture with
H O R I Z O N T A L and **V E R T I C A L**
lines, like Legér's painting.
Add some **dots** and **stripes**,
and some diagonal lines, to make
your pattern really *exciting*.

Peasants Binding Twigs, *by Pieter Bruegel*

Look closer

- The peasants collecting wood are looking watchful, perhaps slightly alarmed. Why do you think they are so alert?
- One of these pictures is 400 years old. Can you guess which one?
- Verbs are doing words, like *lift, carry, pull, push, gather.* Which of these verbs describe activities in which picture?

In the *distance* a man chops thin branches of wood for the other two men to collect and tie into bundles. These twigs will be used as **kindling** wood to get a fire going.

The large man is healthy and strong, while the thin man looks sick and ragged. Perhaps he has a painful toothache!

Relaxing

Holiday, *by James Tissot*

▲ A group of elegantly dressed people are having a picnic beside a garden pond in the shade of a chestnut tree. They look very **relaxed**, sipping tea and resting against the trees or against each other. Do you think the old lady has dozed off with her cup of tea still in her hand? Tissot enjoyed painting beautiful clothes, like the ones the people are wearing in this picture. He painted this scene in his own London garden.

Activity

Make a drawing of four people in contrasting poses. One should look **ENERGETIC**, one should look **busy**, one should look **lazy**, and one should look **relaxed**. When you have finished, ask some friends if they can tell which is which!

These young men are relaxing. One is *lazily* swimming in a cool and shady pool, two are *gently* wrestling on the grass, and some are just *dreaming*. This picture was painted in the artist's studio, but the fresh daylight colors make you think it was painted outdoors. This is just what the artist wanted, to give the impression that he had actually been at the bathing scene.

Look closer

- Look at the arrangement of the glass water bottles on the picnic cloth in *Holiday*. It echoes the shape of the chestnut leaves above. What else is arranged like this?

- Can you find four men, three young women, one old lady, and a child in *Holiday*? Look carefully — they aren't all easy to see!

- In which season was *Holiday* painted? How can you tell?

Summer Scene, *by Jean Frédéric Bazille*

19

Animals

The Forest Fire, *by Piero di Cosimo*

Activity

With friends, make a l o n g picture based on this painting, to put up on the wall. Create a magical forest with paint, and cut out your animals from colored or patterned paper to make a collage. Add as many animals as you like. Imagine and draw your own part animal, part human creatures to live in this strange world.

▲ This painting shows a beautiful country scene on a lovely summer day – and yet something is **wrong**. Fire sweeps through the heart of the forest, while people and animals flee for their lives. Flames and sparks **leap** through the leaves, and smoke **billows** through the branches. The artist made this picture about 500 years ago. He wanted to make the animals and the countryside as important as the people in his paintings, to show that they are all part of the wonders of creation.

20

Look closer

- How many different kinds of animal can you recognize?

- Can you find two strange creatures with animal bodies and human faces?

- Find four places where the forest is on fire.

- Why has the artist painted some animals and birds much smaller than others?

▶ You can clearly see the fear on this animal's face.

Imagined Creatures

This terrifying imaginary monster is carved out of wood. It has a fierce expression with big **staring** eyes. It was part of a house doorpost, and may have been used to **frighten** away evil spirits.

In China, where this picture was made, dragons are imagined as beautiful creatures who bring **good luck**. This dragon is embroidered on a royal robe in colored silk thread. It is decorated with tiny pearls, called seed pearls. Chinese people perform a traditional dance to **honor** the dragon. The dance looks like the **twisting** shape of this dragon's body.

Figure from a House Post,
Maori, New Zealand

Imperial Dragon, *China*

Activity

Draw an amazing dream creature of your own. Think of the different sorts of imaginary beings, such as goblins, giants, pixies and other fairy people, monsters, serpents, and half-human, half-animal creatures.

▶ A unicorn is an imaginary white horse with a single horn in the center of its forehead. Here the swift wild creature has been captured, fenced in, and tied to a tree with a chain and a decorated collar. This is a **woven** picture, called a **tapestry**, which would have been used as a wall hanging in a castle or palace. Some, like this one, have the background covered with flowers. They are called *mille fleur* or "thousand flower" tapestries.

The Unicorn in Captivity, *France*

ook closer

- Can you see that the unicorn's horn is a spiral?
- Was the unicorn injured when it was captured?
- Do you think that the wooden Maori monster is laughing, glaring, making a rude face, or just looking a bit sad?
- How many sharp claws and teeth can you see on the Imperial Dragon?

Spring and Summer

Spring, *by Frederick Walker*

▲ Two children gather primroses. The girl pushes aside budding twigs of pussy willow to reach some hidden flowers. This picture was painted outdoors in spring, in very great **detail**. You can almost see each individual leaf. Although the artist planned the picture carefully, he wanted it to look as if he had **accidentally** captured this charming moment.

On a glorious day during their summer vacation, three of the artist's children are enjoying an idle morning in a rowboat. Elizabeth, Sylvia and George are **dangling** lines into the sea and waiting patiently to catch some fish. The bright light **shimmers** off the water in the **heat** of the sun.

Look closer

- What colors has the artist used to make the shadows in *Calm Morning*?
- Look at the boats. Do you think there is enough breeze for them to sail?
- How many different colors and textures can you find in *Spring*? Notice that the ground is much more than just a plain green carpet of grass.
- Why does the weather look hotter in *Calm Morning* than it does in *Spring*?

Activity

Make a picture of boats with their reflections mirrored in the water, like the sailboats in *Calm Morning*. Choose warm, bright colors for a summer scene and pale, fresh colors for a spring scene.

Calm Morning,
by Frank Weston Benson

Autumn and Winter

Autumn Leaves, *by John Everett Millais*

◀ The artist Millais said he wanted to paint a picture "full of beauty." He chose this glowing autumn scene, in a garden in Scotland. The distant hills look almost purple in the twilight, as Alice, Sophie, Mattie, and Isobella heap the red-gold leaves ready for a bonfire. You can almost **smell** burning leaves when you look at this picture.

Activity

Mix rich, deep warm colors for an autumn picture. You could even stick on some real autumn leaves in beautiful colors and shapes, and paint in colored berries and seeds. Mix cool blues and grays for a winter calendar picture. Make it look so icy that it makes you **shiver** !

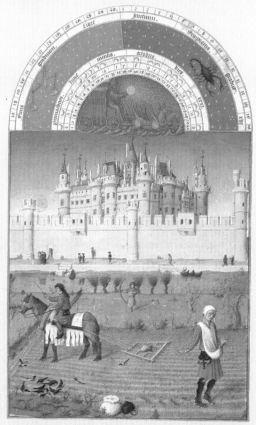

October.
From "Les très riches heures du Duc de Berry"

▶ In this autumn picture farmers are busy sowing seeds for a crop in the spring. The horse pulls a plow to break up the **hard** earth into neat rows. The man in blue **scatters** seed by hand.

26

A Winter's Scene, *by David Teniers*

▲ ***Frozen*** fields meant that little farm work could be done in winter, so people had time to enjoy skating, sledding, and games in the snow. Food was ***scarce***, so the killing of the household pig, shown here, was an important family event. It gave them delicious fresh meat, pies, and sausages to last for months.

▶ The woman with the long-handled pan is waiting to catch the pig's blood. Boys holding straws wait to **burn** the tough hairs off its skin.

Look closer

- The winter scene is painted in *silvery* gray colors, the autumn picture in rich, **glowing** colors. How does each picture make you feel?

- At what time of day do you think that the children are collecting autumn leaves?

- The man in the middle of the *October* picture is actually a scarecrow. Do you think the birds are frightened by his bow and arrow?

Light and Shade

The Starry Night, *by Vincent van Gogh*

Van Gogh was an unhappy and lonely man, but his pictures are full of **energy** and **joy**. Look at the moon detail. See how **thick** the paint is and how **excited** the brushstrokes are. They show color, texture, and pattern all together.

It is night, and the lights are on in the houses of this French village. Above, the deep blue sky *glows* with brilliant stars *whirling* in space. This grand sky makes the dark village look tiny. The tree and the church spire link the earth with the heavens.

Lady Osuma and Sasaya Hanbei,
by Shunkosai Hokuei

These two people are actors in a play. The angry Lady Osuna has been hiding in a cave, waiting to *jump* out and *surprise* the villain of the plot. He looks guilty. The *contrast* is strong between the light from the lantern and the surrounding darkness.

The Fighting Temeraire, *by William Turner*

⏶ "The Fighting Temeraire" was a **warship**. It looks **ghostly** in the sunset. This is a sad scene because the ship is now too old to be useful in battle, and so a tugboat is pulling it along the River Thames to be broken up.

Look closer

- Which picture shows sunlight, firelight, and reflected light?
- Which picture shows starlight and moonlight?
- How have Van Gogh and Turner painted the sky differently?
- What do you think the angry Japanese lady is saying? Can *you* make the expressions on the actors' faces?

⏶ Turner painted with brushes, but he also put paint on with a knife, rags, the ends of his brushes, and even his *hands*!

Activity

Make your own colorful sunset or starry moonlight picture using **THICK** brushstrokes. Experiment with ways to add on paint, like Turner did. Remember to wash your brushes often to keep your colors clear.

Music

The Banjo Lesson, *by Henry Ossawa Tanner*

▲ A boy concentrates on **plucking** the right string on his banjo. It is not easy for him, because he is small and the banjo seems very large. This is probably a father and son together. They seem close and loving, as they share the music lesson in their warm and comfortable kitchen. Look at how the **texture** of the paint in the background gives a lively and interesting feel to the plain walls.

Look closer

- How has the artist made the plain and simple kitchen in the *Banjo Lesson* look *so* cosy?

- In *The Harpsichord Lesson* there are lots of carefully painted details, like the man's earring and the buckle on his belt. Can you find any others?

- Look at the long, thin horn the angel Gabriel is blowing. What sort of sound do you think he is making?

Activity

Listen to a piece of music. What sort of ideas and pictures come into your head? Make a picture of the music. It does not have to look like anything you recognize.

The Harpsichord Lesson,
by Jan Steen

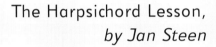

▲ A pretty girl is working hard at her music lesson. She is playing a **harpsichord**, which is a kind of early piano. She is being watched carefully by her teacher, who is pointing to her fingers. This is an ordinary household scene, but the artist has painted it in great detail. He has used a **delicate** and **gentle** color scheme.

◀ The angel Gabriel delivers a musical **fanfare** to announce good news sent from God to humankind. Gabriel strides along purposefully. The feeling of movement and rhythm is made stronger by his flowing wings, floating sashes, and flying hat-trim.

Angel Gabriel, *Egypt or Syria*

Dance

It is night and people are dancing by moonlight beside the sea. The artist has painted the place where she grew up, in Portugal. Memories from her childhood often come into her pictures. This picture is a "dance of life." At first a young girl is alone, then she dances with the man she will marry, and then she dances while she is pregnant with her own child. The three figures dancing in the background show "the three ages of woman."

Activity

Roll out modeling clay into thin strips. On a flat surface make the rubbery strips into people dancing. You can make exaggerated poses easily and change anything in seconds, just as poses change in a dance.

The Dance, *by Paula Rego*

Shield Dance, *by Spencer Asah*

This scene is not as **fierce** as it looks! These members of the Kiowa tribe of Native Americans are acting out a war scene in a dance. These sorts of dances have become a traditional and proud **celebration** of the way they once used to live.

Look closer

- Can you guess at a name for the Native American chiefs by looking at their shields?

- See how the long hair of the Indian god makes a pattern as it floats with the rhythm of the dance.

- How does the artist show that the figures in *The Dance* are dancing, not standing still?

▶ This sculpture shows the Hindu god, Shiva Nataraja, dancing in a circle of fire. He gracefully lifts one foot while crushing a wicked demon with the other. The flames *flickering* around the outside circle look like his fingers twisting and turning as he dances. His many arms create a feeling of movement and *rhythm*. It is not surprising that he is also known as the Lord of the Dance.

Shiva as Nataraja, *India*

Shapes

Swinging,
*by Wassily
Kandinsky*

◀ This picture does not look like anything that we can *recognize* in real life. The artist wanted his glowing colors and beautiful shapes to make us think about our feelings. He believed that *feelings* are as important a subject for paintings as the things we see around us.

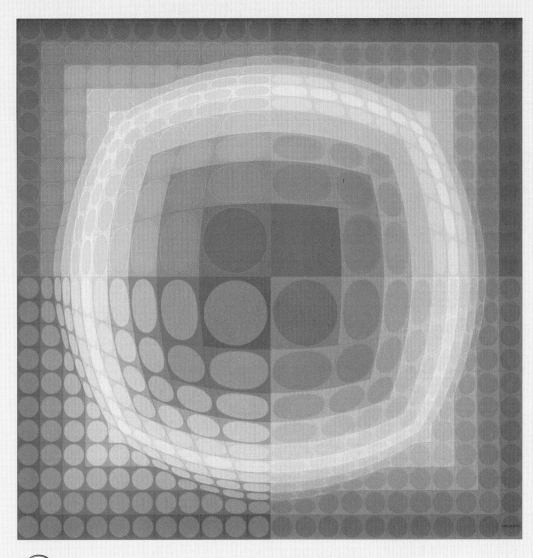

◀ This artist liked to paint pictures that can **trick your eye**. The painting is on a flat surface, yet by cleverly arranging the shapes and colors he makes you think that it is **bulging** in the middle. The design of the picture is perfectly **symmetrical**. This means that the shapes are *identical* on both sides of an invisible line through the center.

Pal-Ket, *by Victor Vasarély*

Look closer

- In *Swinging*, how many rectangles, circles, half circles, and triangles can you find?
- Is there a perfect square in *Swinging*?
- What is the effect of *Pal-Ket* on your eyes? Does the picture seem to be moving?
- Can you see how the artist has squashed some of the circles in *Pal-Ket*? Why do you think he has done this?

Activity

Make a perfectly balanced pattern by painting a design on only half of a sheet of paper. Before the paint dries, fold the paper over so that the design prints on the empty half of the paper. You will then have a **symmetrical** painting!

Patterns

Expectation, *by Gustav Klimt*

◀ The woman in this painting looks mysterious. She is nearly hidden by the **bold** pattern of her clothes and the swirling, curving design of the background. Only her face and hands can be seen as she *gazes* out of the picture looking for some*one* or some*thing*. Klimt made his pictures look like brilliantly colored **mosaics**. He loved to use gleaming gold and silver, perhaps because his father was a silversmith who made designs in precious metals.

Activity

Make a mosaic collage. Cut up lots of small pieces of brightly colored paper, perhaps from magazines, and stick them onto a piece of paper in a patterned design. Add sequins and dots of gleaming glitter-glue for extra shine.

Australian Aboriginal artists used to tell stories about their homeland in sand pictures. This painting uses patterns to show the desert, as if you were looking down on it from above. Circles may be water holes, wavy lines may be rivers or snakes, routes are marked by animal tracks. It may also be a picture of "Dreamtime," which is the Aborigines' way of explaining how the world began.

Possum, Wallaby and Cockatoo Dreaming, *by Michael Jagamara Nelson*

This royal portrait has rich patterns of precious *jewels* and fine *embroidery*, which show the queen's wealth and importance. Her dress is covered with pearls and rubies in a complicated design. It is very *intricate* and would have been very heavy to wear.

Look closer

- How many different textures can you find in the portrait of Queen Elizabeth I?
- The rose in the top left corner of the portrait of Elizabeth is repeated on her dress. Can you find it?
- Can you find hidden in the desert patterns the tracks for the wallaby, the possum, and the cockatoo?
- Can you find the eyes hidden in the pattern of the woman's dress in *Expectation*?

Elizabeth I, *by Nicholas Hilliard*

Letters

One airplane shoots another down in flames – whaam! The artist took the idea for this picture from a comic, because he wanted to create the excitement and energy of a **cartoon**. He has even included a speech bubble. The picture is **huge**, the size of a whole wall in a small room. The strong design and startling bright colors make it an extraordinarily powerful picture.

Whaam!, *by Roy Lichtenstein*

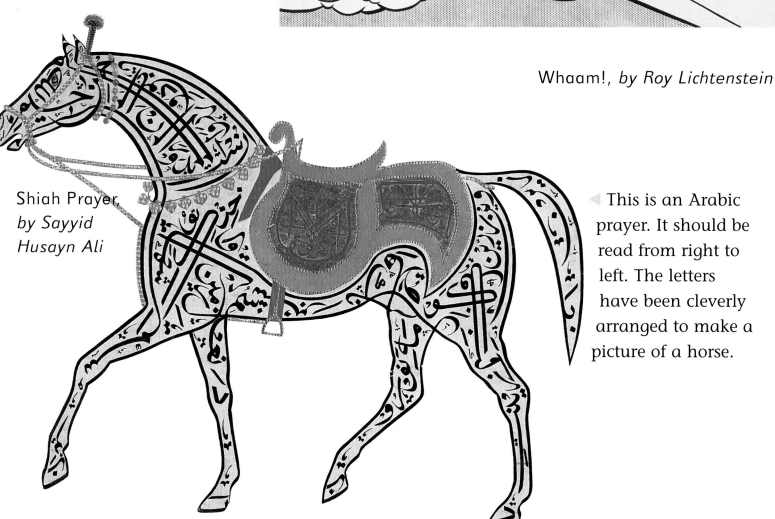

Shiah Prayer, *by Sayyid Husayn Ali*

This is an Arabic prayer. It should be read from right to left. The letters have been cleverly arranged to make a picture of a horse.

Activity

Draw an action-packed picture, with people having a conversation in speech bubbles. Make the words L A R G E and important in the picture.

▼ Letters are **dotted** around in a lively background pattern, on this page from a book. The book contains prayers and bible readings, decorated with beautiful pictures, and was made by *hand* for a woman named Marguerite d'Orléans to use when she prayed alone at home. It is called a "Book of Hours."

Look closer

- Look closely at the background of *Whaam!* Can you see that it is made up of large painted dots? This it to make it look as if it has been printed on a machine.

- In *Whaam!* the shapes are heavily outlined in black. Why do you think the artist has done this?

- Trace the outlines of the horse with your finger. Every line turns into an Arabic letter.

- Long ago quill pens, made from large feathers, were used for writing, and so letters looked different from ours today. Can you recognize all the letters in this book detail?

Heures de Marguerite d'Orléans, *France*

That's Strange

Golconda, *by René Magritte*

Here is a perfectly ordinary street in daytime. But something very odd is happening. From a cloudless blue sky it is raining the strangest rain! The artist has painted things to look as real as possible, but he has added something quite unreal and **impossible**. This reminds us how important are our **dreams** and **imagination**.

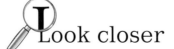ook closer

- The "raining men" above are all dressed in the same way. What do you think their jobs could be?

- Notice the countryside seen through the window next to the grandfather. Do you think the artist has copied it from real life or imagined it?

- The sculpture has interesting shaped holes. Do they make the figure look heavier or lighter? Why?

A grandfather has his arms round his grandson, whose small hand tenderly reaches up to him. The old man looks large and **solid**, while the child seems small and *delicate*. His long wavy hair looks odd to us, but when the picture was painted, about 500 years ago, this was how young boys looked. The strange bumps on the grandfather's face are a skin problem of old age, called "potato nose." The cracks on his forehead are just splits in the paint.

Activity

Ghirlandaio painted his picture with tempera paint. This is powder color mixed with egg yolk to make a creamy, very shiny paint that lasts a long time. Try making a small picture using this mixture — but watch out, it dries hard as a rock in minutes!

Portrait of an Old Man with a Young Boy
by Domenico Ghirlandaio

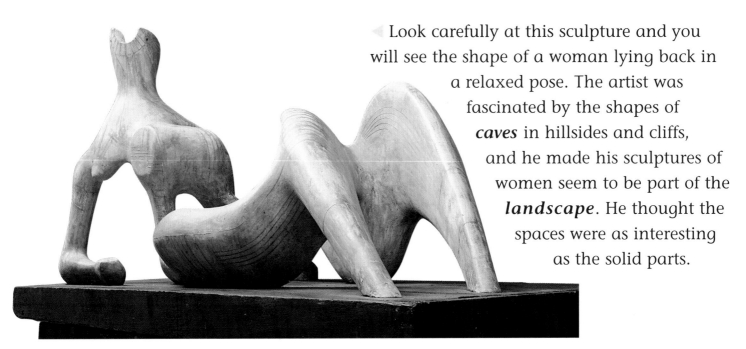

Look carefully at this sculpture and you will see the shape of a woman lying back in a relaxed pose. The artist was fascinated by the shapes of *caves* in hillsides and cliffs, and he made his sculptures of women seem to be part of the *landscape*. He thought the spaces were as interesting as the solid parts.

Reclining Figure, 1951, *by Henry Moore*

Art Detective Quiz

You have now looked at lots of different pictures – but how well do you **remember** them? Be a Picture Detective! Try this quiz to find out how sharp your eyes are. When you've done the quiz yourself, you could try it out on an adult, to test how observant *they* are!

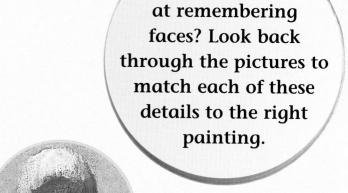

Are you good at remembering faces? Look back through the pictures to match each of these details to the right painting.

Find the Faces!

A portrait is a painting of a real person, not an imagined one. The many portrait faces in this book all have different expressions. Which did you like best? What would your favorite face be saying, if it could speak?

Find the Hands!

Where have you seen these hands before? Look back through the pictures in the book to find out whose they are.

Did you know that even when you are not talking, your hands can give messages to other people, for example when you point, clap, or wave.

How many different kinds of hand gesture can you find in the pictures?

Find the Backgrounds!

Did you notice what was happening in the background of any of the paintings in this book? Let your eye travel around a picture, to look at every single thing the artist has painted. That way, you won't miss anything important.

Which paintings do these background details come from?

Find the Hidden Patterns!

Patterns are all around you. If you look carefully you will see patterns in almost all the works of art in this book. Sometimes they are made by thickly painted brushstrokes, or by the texture of a carving or a sculpture. Perhaps it is the pattern of leaves against the sky, or the folds of someone's clothes.

Which pictures do these pattern details come from? How many more patterns can you find?

43

Picture List

This list tells you when each picture was made, what size it is, who the artist was and what materials they used. It also tells you in which gallery or museum in the world you can see it.

Mother and Child

p. 8 *The Naughty Boy*, 1888
HUBERT VON HERKOMER
oil on canvas 158 x 235 cm
Watford Borough Council Museum

p. 8 *Madonna and Child with the Infant St John (The Taddei Tondo)*, 1504
MICHELANGELO BUONARROTI
Carrara marble relief
104 x 106.5 cm
Royal Academy of Arts, London

p. 9 *The Child's Bath*, 1893
MARY CASSATT
oil on canvas
100.33 x 66 cm
The Art Institute of Chicago, Robert A. Waller Fund

Faces

p. 10 *Portrait of a Lady in Yellow*, c.1465
ALESSO BALDOVINETTI
tempera and oil on wood
62.9 x 40.6 cm
National Gallery, London

p. 10 *Three-Faced Mask*
NIGERIAN, EKOI
Deutsches Leder Museum, Frankfurt

p. 11 *Senecio*, 1922
PAUL KLEE
oil on gauze on cardboard
40.5 x 38 cm
Oeffentliche Kunstsammlung, Basel

Figures

p. 12 *Man Pointing*, 1947
ALBERTO GIACOMETTI
bronze
176.5 x 90 x 62 cm
Tate Gallery, London

p. 12 Detail from *Draped Standing Figures in Red*, 1948
HENRY MOORE
crayon, ink and wash
29.2 x 24.1 cm
Private Collection, U.S.A.

p. 13 *Trooping the Colour*, 1958-9
WILLIAM ROBERTS
oil on canvas
183 x 274 cm
Tate Gallery, London

Moving Figures

p. 14 *The Mud Bath*, 1914
DAVID BOMBERG
oil on canvas
152.5 x 224 cm
Tate Gallery, London

p. 15 *Discus Thrower*, 2nd century
GRECO-ROMAN
marble
height 1650 cm
Townley Collection, British Museum, London

p. 15 *Tanzt Entsetzen*, 1931
PAUL KLEE
pen and colored ink
47.9 x 31.4 cm
Museum of Fine Arts, Boston, Gift of Mr and Mrs Richard K. Weil

Working

p. 16 *The Builders*, 1950
FERNAND LÉGER
oil on canvas
299.8 x 200 cm
Musée National Fernand Léger, Biot, Gift of Nadia Léger and Georges Bauquier

p. 17 *Two Peasants Binding Twigs*, 1500s
PIETER BRUEGEL
oil on wood
36.2 x 27.3 cm
Barber Institute of Fine Arts, University of Birmingham, Edgebaston

Relaxing

p. 18 *Holiday*, c.1876
JAMES TISSOT
oil on canvas
76.2 x 99.4 cm
Tate Gallery, London

p. 19 *Summer Scene*, 1869
JEAN FRÉDÉRIC BAZILLE
oil on canvas
160.02 x 160.66 cm
Courtesy of the Fogg Art Museum, Harvard University Art Museums, Gift of Mr and Mrs F. Meynier de Salinelles

Animals

Imagined Creatures

Spring and Summer

Autumn and Winter

Light and Shade

Music

Dance

Index

Acknowledgements

Licenced by the Aboriginal Artists' Agency/ National Gallery of Australia, Canberra: p 37t purchased with admission charges
Ashmolean Museum, Oxford: p 20-21
Photo Bibliothèque nationale de France, Paris: p 39b
Courtesy of the Museum of Fine Arts Boston: p15tr Klee © DACS, London 1999, p 25 & p 6bl
The Bridgeman Art Library, London: title page, p 16 Léger © ADAGP, Paris and DACS, London 1999, p 17, p 19, p 24, p 26tl, p 26br, p 31t, p 35 Vasarély © ADAGP, Paris and DACS, London 1999, p 33br, p 37b, p 40 Magritte © ADAGP, Paris and DACS, London 1999, p 41t
© The British Museum: p 15bl, p 31b
Photograph © 1998, The Art Institute of Chicago. All Rights Reserved: p 9 & p 7tr Cassatt: Robert A. Waller Fund 1910.2.
Dulwich Picture Gallery, London: back cover, p 27
Deutsches Ledermuseum, Frankfurt: p 10b
Hampton University Museum, Hampton, Virginia: p 30
By kind permission of Paula Rego and Marlborough Fine Art (London) Ltd: p 32
The Metropolitan Museum of Art, New York: p 22 & p 6r The Michael C.Rockefeller Memorial Collection, Bequest of Nelson A. Rockefeller 1979 (1979.206.1508)/Photograph © 1994 The Metropolitan Museum of Art, p 22br Gift of Robert E.Tod, 1929

(29.36)/Photograph © 1980 The Metropolitan Museum of Art, p 23 Gift of John D. Rockefeller, Jr., The Cloisters Collection 1937 (37.80.6)/Photograph © 1993 The Metropolitan Museum of Art
By permission of the Henry Moore Foundation, Hertfordshire: p 12r (HMF 2439), p 41b
The National Gallery, London/Corbis: p 10t, p 29
© 1999 The Museum of Modern Art, New York: p 28 tl and detail p 28 cr
Photo Offentliche Kunstsammlung Basel, Martin Bühler: p 11 Klee © DACS, London 1999
Royal Academy of Arts, London: p 8b & p 6tl & p 7cl
Tate Gallery, London: front cover Matisse © Succession H.Matisse/DACS, London 1999, p 12l Giacometti © ADAGP, Paris and DACS, London 1999, p 13 © Tate Gallery, London, p 18, p 34 Kandinsky © ADAGP, Paris and DACS, London 1999, p 38t © Estate of Roy Lichtenstein/ DACS, London 1999
Photo courtesy of the US Department of the Interior, Indian Arts and Crafts Board, Southern Plains Indian Museum: p 32bl
Victoria and Albert Museum, London V&A Picture Library: p 28bl, p 38b
Watford Borough Council Museum/Photo A.A.Barnes: p 8 & p 7tl